GROSS

WORLD RECORDS

meadowside
CHILDREN'S BOOKS

OLDEST VOMIT

On 12 February 2002, a team of palaeontologists, led by Professor Peter Doyle of Greenwich University, UK, announced their discovery of the fossilized vomit of a marine reptile. Discovered in a quarry in Peterborough, the 160 million-year-old vomit could provide an insight into the feeding habits of ichthyosaurs.

MOST HAND AMPUTATIONS –
SAME ARM

Clint Hallam of New Zealand has had his right hand amputated a total of three times. He first lost his hand in 1984 after an accident with a circular saw. Surgeons managed to re-attach the limb, but an infection developed and it was removed again in 1988. In September 1998, doctors performed a pioneering hand transplant on Clint at a hospital in Lyons, France. However, Mr Hallam later requested that it be amputated again. This took place at a London hospital on 2 February 2001.

MOST COMMON SKIN INFECTION

Tinea Pedis, commonly known as 'Athlete's foot', is the most common skin infection in humans. The fungus afflicts up to 70% of the worldwide population and almost everyone will get it at least once in their lifetime. The infection manifests when the skin between the toes becomes soft and peels away, and it may even crack and ooze.

MOST BLOODTHIRSTY PARASITE

The indistinguishable eggs of the hookworms *Ancylostoma duodenale* and *Necator americanus* are found in the faeces of 1.3 billion people worldwide. In cases of heavy infestation, the lining of the gut is so thickly covered with worms that they look like the pile of a carpet. The bleeding that results from their feeding adds up to a total of 10 million litres (2.6 million gallons) of blood worldwide every day.

HEAVIEST GUT-BARGING CONTESTANT

Gut barger David George White, aka 'Mad Maurice Vanderkirkoff', from Trowbridge, Wiltshire, UK, weighed in at 141.5 kg (312 lb) with a gut circumference of 137.7 cm (54.25 in) on the set of *Guinness World Records: Primetime*, Los Angeles, USA, on 12 March 2001.

MOST FEET AND ARMPITS SNIFFED

Madeline Albrecht was employed at the Hill Top Research Laboratories in Cincinnati, Ohio, USA, a testing lab for products by Dr Scholl. She worked there for 15 years and had to smell approximately 5,600 feet and an indeterminate number of armpits.

LARGEST PARASITE.

The broad or fish tapeworm, *Diphyllobothrium latum*, inhabiting the small intestine of fishes and sometimes humans too, attains a length of 9.1–12.1 m (30–40 ft) but can exceptionally reach 18.3 m (60 ft). It has been estimated that if a specimen survived for ten years, it could possess a chain of segments (proglottids) measuring almost 8 km (5 miles) long and containing two billion eggs!

MOST WORMS REMOVED FROM A HUMAN STOMACH

A 58-year-old woman from Shizuoka, Japan, was admitted to Isogaki Gastro-Entero-Surgical clinic in May 1990. She complained of severe gastric pain and nausea brought on by eating sashimi (sliced raw fish). Doctors discovered 56 white, thread-like worms in her stomach and later removed them during a 90-min operation. The worms were identified as the larvae of *Anisakis simplex* and measured up to 17.27 mm (0.67 in) in length.

MOST WORMS EATEN IN 30 SEC

Mark Hogg (USA) swallowed a total of
94 night crawlers in 30 sec on the set of the
Regis Philbin Show (KGTV-TV, USA) in
October 2000.

LONGEST EAR HAIR

Radhakant Bajpai (India) has hair sprouting from the centre of his outer ears (middle of the pinna) that measures 13.2 cm (5.19 in) at its longest point.

HEAVIEST OBJECT SWALLOWED

The heaviest object extracted from a human stomach was a ball of hair weighing 2.53 kg (5 lb 3 oz) from a 20-year-old female compulsive swallower in the South Devon and East Cornwall Hospital, UK, on 30 March 1895.

LARGEST OBJECT REMOVED FROM A HUMAN SKULL

The largest object removed from a human skull is a 20.32 cm (8 in) survival knife with a serrated blade, which had been plunged into the head of 41-year-old Michael Hill of Jacksonville, Florida, USA, on 25 April 1998.

LOUDEST BURP

Paul Hunn, of Edmonton, London, UK, registered a burp at 118.1 decibels on the set of *Guinness World Records*, London, on 5 April 2000.

FARTHEST EYEBALL POPPER

Kim Goodman of Chicago, Illinois, USA, can pop her eyeballs to a protrusion of 11 mm (0.43 in) beyond her eye sockets. Her eyes were measured on the set of the television show *Guinness World Records: Primetime* on 13 June 1998.

FARTHEST DISTANCE TO SPIT
A CRICKET

Danny Capps of Madison, Wisconsin, USA, spat a dead cricket from his mouth a distance of 9.17 m (30 ft 1.2 in) on the set of *Guinness World Records: Primetime*, Los Angeles, California, USA, on 26 June 1998.

MOST RATS SERVED IN A RESTAURANT

The Jailu Restaurant in Canton, China, serves approximately 9,300 rats every year to its customers. Self-proclaimed rat king and restaurateur Quang Li-Do has been catching and eating rats for 30 years.

MOST BODY PIERCINGS WITH SURGICAL NEEDLES

Ben Moffat (Canada) inserted into his body 700 surgical needles, all 18 gauge (1.2 cm or 0.47 in long), in 7 hr 19 min at Metamorphosis Custom Piercing and Tattoo in Winnipeg, Manitoba, Canada, on 15 January 2003.

LONGEST FINGERNAILS

The aggregate measurement of the five nails on the left hand of Shridhar Chillal (India) was 6.15 m (20 ft 2.25 in) when measured on the set of *Guinness World Records: Primetime*, Los Angeles, California, USA on 8 July 1998.
His thumb measured 142.24 cm (56 in), his index finger 109.22 cm (43 in), his middle finger 117.47 cm (46.25 in), his ring finger 125.73 cm (49.5 in) and his little finger 120.65 cm (47.5 in).
Chillal last cut his fingernails in 1952.

LARGEST WAIST

The largest waist on record was that of
Walter Hudson (USA), which measured
302 cm (119 in) at his peak weight of
545 kg (85 st 7 lb).

STRETCHIEST SKIN

Garry Turner, of Caistor, Lincolnshire, UK, stretched the skin of his stomach a measured length of 15.8 cm (6.25 in) on the set of *Guinness World Records: Primetime* in Los Angeles, California, USA, on 29 October 1999.

WORST FLESH-EATING DISEASE

Dubbed the 'flesh-eating bug' by the press in May 1994, *necrotizing fasciitis*, the rare and deadly 'flesh-eating' disease, has been around since World War I. The cunning *Streptococcus* bacteria which causes the disease first attacks a layer of tissue below the skin, leaving gangrene in its wake for which there is only one cure – surgical removal of the infected area.

LARGEST TUMOUR REMOVED INTACT

The largest tumour removed intact was a multicystic mass of the right ovary weighing 137.6 kg (303 lb). The operation, which took over six hours, was performed by Professor Katherine O'Hanlan of Stanford University Medical Center, California, USA. Tests later revealed that the benign tumour was mostly fluid, although teeth and hair were found growing inside.

LONGEST SOLID OBJECT
SWALLOWED BY A DOG

Kyle, a collie/Staffordshire bull terrier, who
is 45.7 cm (18 in) long, swallowed a
38.1-cm (15-in) long bread knife in
December 2000. The knife was stuck in its
stomach, pointing towards its throat.

MOST PIERCED WOMAN

In January 1997, Elaine Davidson of
Edinburgh, UK, had her first body piercing.
As of May 2003, the total had risen to a
record-breaking 1,500 piercings all
over her body.

MOST SCORPIONS EATEN

The most live scorpions eaten in a lifetime
by a human is approximately 35,000, by
field worker Rene Alvarenga, aka
'El comealacranes' (scorpion eater), of
Intipuca, El Salvador. He catches them with
his bare hands and eats them live.
He eats about 20–30 per day.

MOST COCKROACHES EATEN

Ken Edwards of Glossop, Derbyshire, UK, ate 36 cockroaches in one minute on the set of *The Big Breakfast* (Channel 4, UK), London, UK, on 5 March 2001.

MOST LIVE COCKROACHES HELD IN THE MOUTH

John LaMedica of Newark, Delaware, USA, held six Hissing Madagascan cockroaches in his mouth for 10 sec on 5 December 2001 at the television studios of *Ricki Lake* in New York, USA.

MOST COCKROACHES IN A COFFIN

'Jungle' John LaMedica, of Newark, Delaware, USA, was placed in a plexiglass coffin and had 20,050 Giant Madagascan Hissing cockroaches poured over him on 12 August 1999, on the set of *Guinness World Records: Primetime*, Hollywood, California, USA.

OLDEST UNDISCOVERED TWIN

In July 1997, a foetus was discovered in the abdomen of 16-year-old Hisham Ragab (Egypt), who had been complaining of stomach pains. A swollen sac found pressing against his kidneys turned out to be Hisham's 18-cm (7-in) long, 2-kg (4-lb 6-oz) identical twin. The foetus, which had been growing inside him, had lived to the age of 32 or 33 weeks.

SMELLIEST SUBSTANCE

Two substances called 'Who Me?' and 'The US Government Standard Bathroom Malodor' are jointly recognized as the world's smelliest substances. The US Government is currently investigating military applications of these substances. It is thought they could be used as giant stink bombs to disperse rioting crowds or separate warring factions.

MOST BIG MACS CONSUMED

Donald Gorske (USA) holds the record for the most Big Macs consumed. By 7 March 2002, Donald had consumed a total of 18,250 of McDonalds' largest burgers – eating 708 in 2000 alone. He began his quest in 1972 with nine Big Macs a day and is quick to tell people that he eats Big Macs because he loves them. 'Being able to eat Big Macs after work, everyday, is one of my favourite things,' he said. 'And my body weight is the same now as it was 28 years ago.'

LARGEST CHEST MEASUREMENT

Circus and sideshow performer Robert Earl Hughes (USA) had a chest measurement of 315 cm (124 in). At his death in 1958, he topped the scales at an amazing 484 kg (1,067 lb) and was buried in a coffin the size of a piano case.

LONGEST LEG HAIR

A hair grown just below the knee of the right leg of Julian Rowe (UK) reached a length of 10.1 cm (3.97 in) long when measured at The Cathedral High School, Wakefield, West Yorkshire, UK, on 2 July 2002.

LARGEST APPENDIX REMOVED

An appendix removed from Spencer Bayles (UK) on 2 November 2002 at Lister Hospital, Stevenage, Hertfordshire, UK, measured 21 cm (8.26 in) in length.

LARGEST SEWAGE WORKS

The Stickney Water Reclamation Plant
(formerly the West-Southwest Sewage
Treatment Works), Stickney, Illinois, USA,
began operation in 1939 on a site covering
231 ha (570 acres) in suburban Chicago,
Illinois, USA. With a design capacity of
5.44 billion litres (1.2 billion gallons) per
day, it treated an average of 3.03 billion
litres (668 million gallons) of water
per day in 1995.

OLDEST DISEASE

Cases of leprosy were described in ancient Egypt as early as 1350 BC. *Tuberculosis schistosomiasi*, an infectious disease of the lungs, has also been seen in Egyptian mummies from the twentieth dynasty (1250 to 1000 BC). The plague and cholera are both referred to in the Old Testament.

MOST LEPERS CURED

In the 15 years between 1983 and 1998,
almost 10 million people were cured of
leprosy – part of a concerted effort to
eliminate the disease by 2000.

MOST MILKSHAKE DISPENSED THROUGH THE NOSE

Gary Bashaw, Jr of Barr, West Virginia, USA, mixed milk and chocolate powder in his mouth, and dispensed the chocolate milk mixture measuring 54 ml (1.82 oz) from his nostril, on the set of *Guinness World Records: Primetime* in Los Angeles, California, USA, in August 1999.

FARTHEST MARSHMALLOW NOSE-BLOW

The farthest a marshmallow has been blown out of one nostril and caught in the mouth of a catcher is 4.96 m (16 ft 3.5 in), by Scott Jeckel (launcher) of Delavan, Illinois, USA, and Ray Perisin (catcher), of Peoria, Illinois, USA, on the set of *Guinness World Records: Primetime* in Los Angeles, California, USA, on 13 August 1999.

FARTHEST NASAL EJECTION
(SPAGHETTI)

Kevin Cole of Carlsbad, New Mexico, USA, holds the record for the longest spaghetti strand ejected from a nostril in a single blow. On 16 December 1998, Cole successfully achieved a record length of 19 cm (7.5 in) on the set of *Guinness World Records: Primetime* in Los Angeles, California, USA.

LONGEST MILK SQUIRT FROM THE EYE

Mike Moraal of Vancouver, British Columbia, Canada, squirted milk from his eye a distance of 2.615 m (8.71 ft) on the set of *L'Émission des Records*, Paris, France, on 7 September 2001.

CASH
DISPENSER

MOST COINS REGURGITATED ON REQUEST

Stevie Starr (UK) swallowed 11 Spanish 100-peseta coins, each with a different year of minting, and regurgitated them on request from 11 different members of the studio audience at *El Show de los Récords*, Madrid, Spain, on 5 December 2001.

MOST PEOPLE SIMULTANEOUSLY SLIMED

On 12 March 1999, 731 people were simultaneously slimed when two suspended tanks containing a total of 1,669 litres (368 gallons) of bright yellow slime were dumped on top of the willing crowd, in Birmingham, UK. All slime victims had gathered to raise money for Comic Relief.

MOST PROLIFIC CANNIBAL

During the 19th century, the hungriest
cannibal, Ratu Udre Udre, reportedly ate
between 872 and 999 people. The Fijian
chief had kept a stone to record each body
eaten, and these were placed along his
tomb in Rakiraki, northern Viti Levu, Fiji.

LARGEST TICK

Hard ticks, members of the suborder
Ixodida, are blood-sucking, eight-legged
parasites that can expand to 30 mm
(1.4 in) – the size of a large walnut – to
accommodate the volume of blood
they require to survive.

LARGEST MAMMAL EXPLODED

The largest mammal ever exploded was the 13.7-m (45-ft) long carcass of a sperm whale washed up south of Florence, Oregon, USA. On 12 November 1970, the Oregon State Highway Division placed half a tonne of dynamite around the foul-smelling whale and detonated it. Numerous spectators gathered to see the sight, but when the dynamite was detonated they found themselves being pelted by large pieces of rotten blubber. One man-sized chunk of whale meat crushed the roof of a Buick car a quarter of a mile away.

HYDRONEPHROSIS – MOST FLUID REMOVED

A 35-year-old patient diagnosed with hydronephrosis – an enlargement of the kidney caused by a blockage to normal urine flow – at Bugshan Hospital, Jeddah, Saudi Arabia, had 22 litres (38.7 pints) of urine removed from his kidney on 16 June 1999. The normal capacity is 3–5 ml (0.105–0.175 fl oz) of urine. The kidney was eventually removed on 6 July 1999 and measured 50 x 40 x 25 cm (19.6 x 15.7 x 9.8 in) and weighed 700 g (24.6 oz).

For even **more**
fascinating
facts...

100s of
new
records!

ALL NEW
pictures!

www.guinnessworldrecords.com

Cartoons by:
Guy Harvey

Designed and edited by:
Jon Richards, Ed Simkins

For Guinness World Records:
Claire Folkard, Craig Glenday,
Kim Lacey, Christian Marais

Printed in India